W.

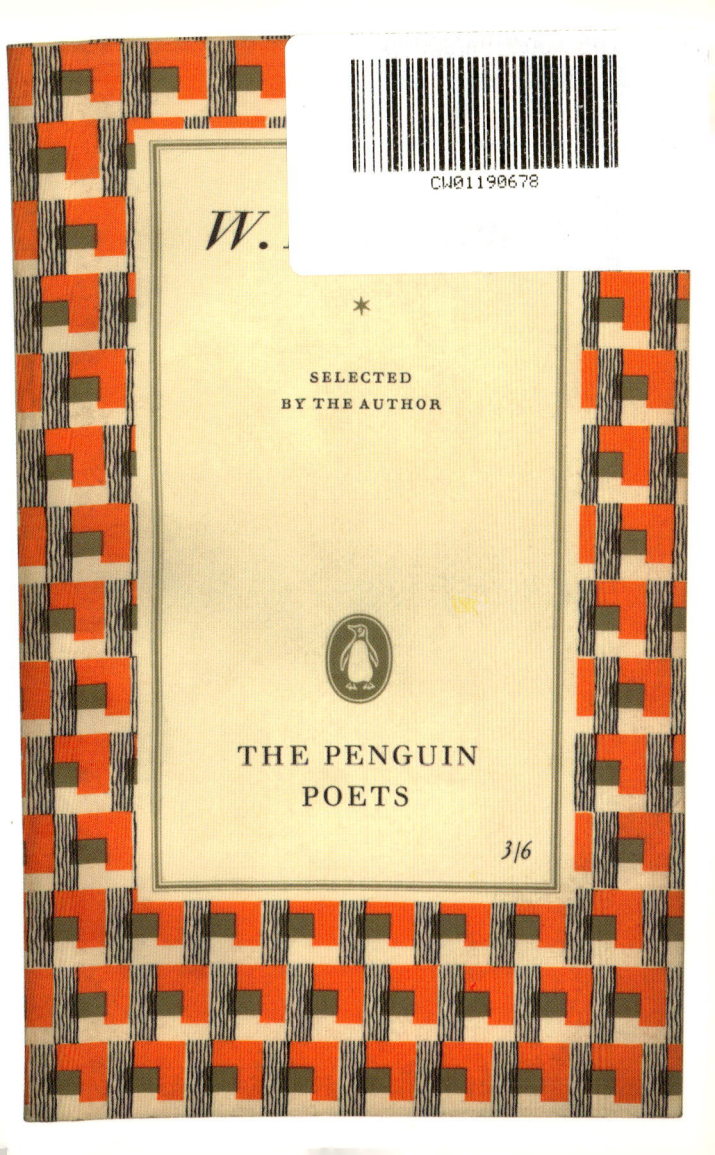

SELECTED
BY THE AUTHOR

THE PENGUIN
POETS

3/6

# POST CARD
### CARTE POSTALE

I've included 4 specials, one in each category: fiction, essay/memoir and history.

Hope you enjoy!

menfi

*The Penguin Poets: W. H. Auden, 1958*

# CONTENTS

Introduction
      The Expected and the Unexpected .................... 1
I     Tibet and Manchukuo ......................................... 9
II    A Wall and a Massacre ...................................... 18
III   Orwell and Huxley ............................................ 24
IV   China and Russia .............................................. 42
V    Yu Hua and Mark Twain ................................... 50
VI   Chicken or Beef ................................................. 65
VII  The Flat and the Bumpy .................................... 69
VIII The People's Pope and Big Daddy Xi ................ 76

*Notes* ........................................................................ 86
*Acknowledgements* ..................................................... 89

*This book is dedicated to Tom Lutz, the most energetic 'loafer' I've ever known, and all those who have joined him in making the* Los Angeles Review of Books *such a special foray into the public sphere.*

# INTRODUCTION

## The Expected and the Unexpected

The two-fold premise of this book is simple. First, as the country continues to leapfrog up global hierarchies, it is more important than ever to have illuminating lenses through which to view the People's Republic of China (PRC) – particularly ones that help us make sense of the ways it has changed since 2008, the year Beijing hosted the Olympic Games, an event that transfixed the world's attention. And, second, unconventional forays into comparison can further enrich our understanding of these changes. One reason I put such faith in essays framed around juxtaposition is that I have learned so much over the years from mulling fanciful and curious analogies of my own, and learning from those that others have proposed to me that were either wholly unexpected or gave a radical twist to an expected comparison.

One case in point that has long stuck with me and illustrated the value of the unexpected occurred in

Sweden more than a decade ago when the host of a student radio show, who knew I would be giving a talk about Chinese and American approaches to human rights, asked me if I planned to say much about the human rights issue that many Swedes felt linked the two countries most. I said that I wasn't sure. One theme I was going to bring up, I told her, was a point of contrast: the emphasis that the American government often places on civil and religious rights versus the emphasis that the Chinese state often places on social and economic ones. I was going to move from there to noting a similarity: that both sides stress some parts of the UN's Universal Declaration of Human Rights more than others.

That wasn't what she had in mind, she said. She was thinking of the fact that China and the United States are two of the only major powers in the world that still execute people.

What follows are eight efforts to illustrate how comparing a country often thought of as completely exceptional, rather than only unusual in specific ways, can benefit and invigorate our understanding of China. Some chapters use *unexpected* juxtapositions: in one, for example, I place Xi Jinping beside the Pope and suggest that the two leaders, who assumed power at the same moment, have much in common, even though the former leads an atheist government, the latter a religious order. Other chapters take *conventional* juxtapositions but give them unusual twists. One essay, for instance, places the Tiananmen protests of 1989 beside that year's transformations in Eastern Europe, but rather than assuming that the fall of the Berlin Wall weakened the position of the Chinese Communist Party (CCP), the essay suggests that the tumbling of this Cold War symbol may have actually extended that organisation's lifespan.

Alternately serious and playful in tone, the chapters to come, which draw on experience gained during almost three decades of travelling to and writing and teaching about China, are not offered up as the last word on any topic. Rather, they strive to encourage fresh thinking among readers, while entertaining and describing some key developments of the last eight years – an unusually eventful and consequential stretch of modern Chinese history.

As the period in question commenced, the PRC was the object of intense international interest for a mix of expected and unexpected reasons. Anticipation was rife; 2008 was destined to draw attention to China as the country prepared to host its first Olympics. The resulting spectacle lived up to its promise with an opening ceremony that dazzled audiences around the world. In terms of the unforeseeable, the year saw a massive earthquake rock Sichuan Province and unrest break out in Tibet. Since then, though international interest in China has not always been quite as strong, the country has never been out of the global spotlight for more than a few months at a time. Keeping the country firmly in the headlines was everything from planned spectacles, such as the 2010 Shanghai Expo, to largely unanticipated events, including the 2009 riots in Xinjiang, the 2014 Umbrella Movement in Hong Kong, and the 2015 Shanghai stock market dive.

In addition to being a source of fascination and sometimes concern, Chinese developments of the last eight years have generated a good deal of confusion. What should we think about a place that is run by a Communist Party yet encourages consumerism and had the gall to denounce the protests in Hong Kong, in part, for being bad for business? What should we make of its current leader praising Mao Zedong with one breath and quoting Confucius with the next, even though the former claimed that the latter was a 'feudal' and patriarchal thinker whose ideas had prevented China from modernising and unfairly kept women subservient to men? What does it mean that concern has shifted in many quarters from worrying over whether China will ever be able to 'modernise' to debating what it means for the world and for ordinary Chinese citizens now that it *has* modernised in its own way? And what are the implications of the fact that, for the first time since the days of Chairman

Mao and Deng Xiaoping, the CCP has a leader who, unlike the comparatively colourless Jiang Zemin and Hu Jintao, inspires intense personal devotion among many and is tied to a slogan, 'The Chinese Dream', which is memorable and evocative, if also somewhat vague?

I do not try here to answer questions like these directly, nor to provide a comprehensive picture of this pivotal period. Rather, I seek to illuminate some of the period's key political and cultural contours via commentaries that are each linked to a specific year yet also bring in other parts of the period as well. My hope is that, when taken together, the analogies and comparisons brought into play during this journey across the eight years will work to dispel the lingering hold of outmoded assumptions about China and help readers to look at this shape-shifting country in fresh ways.

Especially since I was pleasantly surprised by that Swedish student radio host, I have been interested in bringing juxtapositions into my own writing and public talks about China, as well as in finding ways to use them that challenge my readers and audiences. For example, I sometimes get asked why Chairman Mao's face appears on Chinese banknotes when he was responsible for such horrors as the famine caused by the Great Leap Forward. When this question is posed to me in the United States, I say that it is indeed very hard to understand how a country would put on its money the visage of a past leader who was responsible for terrible deeds, but that sometimes this happens – and then I project not a shot of a Chinese banknote but a twenty dollar bill, which features the face of a pre-Civil War era president who, while he continues to be rightly admired for some things, is also associated with attitudes most Americans now see as vilely racist and policies toward Native Americans that many now view as genocidal. In showing Andrew Jackson's face, my goal is not, as I explain, to suggest that he and Mao are completely equivalent figures, but rather to unsettle any notion that in having the latter on its bills, China is completely anomalous. I describe this as a useful example of what I refer to in a later chapter as an 'imperfect analogy', which places side-by-side two different yet comparable elements to help us think about each in a new way.

There is a particular value in bringing 'imperfect analogies' into discussions of contemporary China. This is because of two aspects that often hinder clear-sighted views of the country. One is a sense that China is somehow so exotic, singular, or special that it cannot be compared to any other place. The other is a frequent insistence that, while comparisons may be drawn, this should only be done very carefully and by placing it into a single, very specific framework for comparison – such as tracing parallels between the PRC and other 'Communist' states, or between other countries shaped by 'Confucian' values. Visions of China as utterly unique – and as such an entity open to just one specific comparison at a time – have a tenacious hold, as high profile Western works and Chinese government pronouncements reinforce them. If I succeed in my goal, the reader will in the future greet with great scepticism all such statements, whether in books by the likes of Henry Kissinger or in speeches by Xi Jinping, both of which treat China as a thoroughly incomparable place of 'five thousand years of continuous history', and as a country that can only be understood through a single sort of comparative mode.

There is no way to know what will happen next in China, whose course has so often defied the best guesses of prognosticators. We can, though, strive to be better prepared to make sense of what happens there, even when it surprises us. A valuable first step in this direction is to shake off the hold of one-frame comparisons and embrace the juxtapositions we face in understanding China.

# I

# Tibet and Manchukuo

The Chinese government's plans for its long-awaited first turn at hosting the Olympic Games encompassed many detailed preparations, from the building of stadiums to the staging of a grand opening ceremony pageant. A revolt in Tibet was not in the plan. That is, however, just what the CCP got on 14 March 2008, when protests broke out in Lhasa, sparking a movement that eventually affected a giant swath of Tibetan-inhabited land stretching across the Tibetan Autonomous Region to Gansu, Qinghai and Sichuan provinces to the east. In the wake of these demonstrations and riots, the authorities made intensive efforts to restore control over the affected areas and manage access to information about what had happened. The limited effectiveness of this strategy was revealed when, in the wake of the protests, a disruption was caused by some monks at the Jokhang temple in Lhasa during a choreographed visit by foreign journalists.

Beijing's worried officials were determined to defuse the potential of the protests to subvert their larger plans for what the Olympics would mean for China. It is notable in this respect that Chinese officials avoided mentioning the precedent of the 1964 Tokyo Olympic Games, or voicing any sense that there might be a parallel in the impact of these respective events on the global profiles of the host countries. In principle, one attractive way for Beijing authorities to regard the 2008 games was that they would come to be seen as accomplishing for China what the 1964 Olympics had for Japan. The Tokyo games – and the Osaka World Expo that followed in 1970 – promoted a vision of a Japan that had bounced back from a period of extremism and defeat to become a stable country with modern cities and forward-looking aspirations. These two high-profile international gatherings also symbolised the concurrent economic development that would see Japan become the world's second biggest economy.

China's leaders might have, at least in private, considered the Tokyo 1964/Beijing 2008 analogy compelling on several levels – even if their suspicion of a historic adversary (and present competitor) made them reluctant to voice this sentiment openly. China, too, had been rapidly climbing the global economic hierarchy and wanted to move higher still. It was preparing to follow its turn at the Olympics with its own Expo – set to start in Shanghai on 1 May 2010 and be the country's first ever World's Fair. China's own modern history had seen moments of such destructive extremism (the Great Leap Forward) and defeat (Japanese invasions in the 1930s) that, by 2008, it had good reason to want to put those experiences far behind it.

At the same time, if the focus were on Tibet rather than the Games, then a very different analogy could be drawn between China and Japan – one far less palatable than an international sporting event. This was because, as commentators such as the journalist Howard French and the public intellectual Pankaj Mishra argued in 2008, in the *International Herald Tribune* and the *Guardian*, respectively, the era in Japanese history that seemed most relevant for thinking about Beijing's policies toward Tibet was the 1930s – a decade that is remembered by many Chinese as one in which Japan acted in despicably aggressive ways toward its neighbours.[1]

French's background of living in and writing about Africa, a continent that has been ravaged by many forms of imperialism, may have informed his emphasis on a time when Japan was an imperial rather than a post-imperial power, which allowed him to highlight the colonialist aspects of Chinese policy in Tibet. Whatever the route that got him there, in so doing, he evaded the common trap in commenting on Tibet that Mishra identified: namely, that of viewing any confrontation between the Chinese leadership and those challenging its policies through a distorting Cold War lens, which encourages the viewer to think only of analogies between the PRC and other Communist Party-run states.

For both these authors, the place to start when seeking to unravel the Tibetan crisis was not with communist ideology or Leninist state structures. It was, rather, with appreciating what often happens when any power justifies its control by saying that it is bestowing modernity on a backward people – a view of Tibetans held by many Chinese citizens belonging to the country's majority Han ethnic group as well as their (also Han) rulers.

Beijing insistently claimed in 2008 – and would assert even more loudly in September 2015 during official celebrations to mark the fiftieth anniversary of Tibet's conferment as an 'autonomous' part of the PRC – to be delivering the benefits of progress and modernity to Tibetans. This is also something that it has long claimed to be doing for the Uyghurs of Xinjiang, a neighbouring frontier zone roiled by waves of violence in recent years. The recurrent problem the CCP faces is that (in French's words) 'few indigenous people want progress "given" to them'. This is not only because 'they don't see themselves as inferior, as such patronage would require', but also because 'they know of the many strings attached and of the slippery road to losing one's soul'.

More specifically, according to French, the 'Chinese,

of all people, would understand' the outrage that colonial projects of this sort can engender. After all, they were 'offered the "gift" of modernization by Imperial Japan under its erstwhile Greater East Asia Co-Prosperity Sphere'. In this structure, as in the PRC vision of a country under the iron-fist of Beijing (yet with so-called 'autonomy' for Tibetans and Uyghurs in designated locales), Tokyo would mask its colonial structure by setting up pseudo-states that lacked real independence and were represented by handpicked, compliant figureheads. Singling out the most famous controlled ruler of the Greater East Asia Co-Prosperity Sphere, the Last Emperor of the Qing Dynasty (1644–1912), who had abdicated his Beijing throne as a boy and then more than two decades later been drafted by Tokyo to represent his familial homeland of Manchuria in China's far northeast, French wrote of hearing 'eerie echoes of Japan's Manchukuo with its bogus Emperor Puyi in China's attempts to pick religious leaders on Tibetan's behalf'.

The Chinese regime's official *Xinhua* news agency seemed to confirm the thrust of this argument by issuing a statement on 22 March that inadvertently buttressed the Manchukuo parallel. The piece – entitled 'China Garners Broad International Support Over Tibet Riots' – provided a list of countries that had issued official declarations expressing solidarity with Beijing over its handling of Tibet; they ranged from nearby lands such as North Korea and Kyrgyzstan to distant ones such as Syria and Serbia.[2] The list is curiously reminiscent of ones the Japanese authorities and rulers of Manchukuo circulated in the 1930s when trying to convince local and international populations that the newly formed state was widely viewed as legitimate. To distract attention from all of the statements by world leaders dismissing Puyi as a puppet of Japan, those 1930s pronouncements trotted out a list of eleven countries – Poland, El Salvador, Romania, and Spain, among them – that recognised him as a legitimate ruler.

But lest anyone jump to the conclusion that there is something distinctively 'East Asian' about this particular ploy, it is worth remembering what George W. Bush, who would be among the global leaders sitting in the stands when the Beijing games began, did in 2003: namely, use smoke and mirrors to talk of a broad 'coalition of the willing' to encourage people to overlook the lack of United Nations support for the invasion of Iraq. It is interesting, too, to see how much the set of countries that lined up behind Washington in 2003 was consistent with the set that once viewed Puyi as a true ruler rather than a puppet. The above-mentioned four states – Poland, El Salvador, Romania and Spain – were all there again, for example, notwithstanding the great discontinuities in their own political development across the decades.

George W. Bush belatedly expressed concern over the Sichuan earthquake and also discussed events in Tibet in a lengthy phone conversation with his Chinese counterpart, Hu Jintao, who then held the posts of both head of the CCP and President of the PRC.[3] It seems doubtful that their conversation dealt with history. Still, one could imagine that if it had, a relevant topic on which they could have found common ground was the troublesome nature of historical analogies involving 1930s Japan.

To the Bush administration, if there was a Japanese analogy worth drawing on with regards to contemporary US policy, it was with post-war Japan. The influential neo-conservatives who provided the Iraq adventure with ideological varnish built upon the strained but prevalent comparison of 9/11 to Pearl Harbor by arguing that the American occupation of Japan led to the emergence of a grateful democratic ally, and therefore provided a preview of what would happen after Saddam Hussein fell. There would, in this fantasy, be a twenty-first century counterpart to General MacArthur, leader of American forces in Japan following its World War II surrender, and Iraqis who would welcome foreign troops as liberators.

This notion was always problematic, and anyone who really knew their history would not have expected events on the ground in Iraq to follow the blueprint of the American occupation of Japan. John Dower, the leading

American historian of mid-century US-Japanese interaction, expressed such a view in various periodicals just before and during the early stages of the invasion – most notably in 'A Warning from History', which ran in the *Boston Review* – highlighting a host of ways in which the situation in Iraq differed from that in post-war Japan.[4]

Dower then went a step further and argued that the best Japanese parallels for US policy and rhetoric regarding the Middle East in the twenty-first century lay in how much Bush and company had in common with the militarists who led Japan in the 1930s. As he wrote in 2003, 'Regime change, nation-building, creation of client states, control of strategic resources, defiance of international criticism, mobilization for "total war," clash-of-civilizations rhetoric, winning hearts and minds, combating terror at home as well as abroad – all these were part and parcel of Japan's vainglorious attempt to create a new order of "co-existence and co-prosperity" in Asia.'[5]

I doubt that Bush and Hu said much of anything to one another in Beijing while the 2008 games were underway. If they did, though, the subject matter of their conversation was more likely to focus on speed times in swimming races than Pu Yi's similarities to the Panchen Lama; it more likely addressed which country headed the medals table than parallels between American actions in Iraq and Japan's in Manchukuo.

That is a pity, since a modicum of historical self-awareness – especially among the powerful – can be one of the best defences against political misjudgement. But even if the exchange between the leaders of an actual and an aspiring global power remained focused only on current affairs, they could have found some common ground. Each man, thinking of different quagmires – for Bush there was Afghanistan and Iraq, while for Hu there was Xinjiang and Tibet – could have commiserated with the other about how vexing it can be when people you 'liberate' aren't properly grateful for what you have done for them.

# II

# A Wall and a Massacre

What is it about years that end in the numeral 9, when it comes to turning points in the history of Communism? This thought struck me in 2009, when, in rapid succession, a sixtieth anniversary was marked in Beijing and a twentieth anniversary was marked in Berlin. The tone of the commemorative activity in both cases was jubilation, but the events whose anniversaries were being marked could hardly have been more dissimilar. On 1 October, in Beijing, there were massive festivities, including a parade directed by acclaimed filmmaker-turned-state-choreographer Zhang Yimou, the same man responsible for the eye-popping opening ceremony of the 2008 Olympics. Then, in early November, events were held in Germany to remember the fall of the Berlin Wall and the obliteration of the Iron Curtain in Eastern Europe.

This conjuncture of commemorations made the autumn of 2009 an interesting time to reflect on the perils of prediction. Growing up during the Cold War, it seemed to me as if the Berlin Wall and the divisions it symbolised might last forever. The CCP, however, looked doomed to die by the early 1990s, after the 1989 Tiananmen Square uprising and the June Fourth massacre that crushed it triggered a massive legitimacy crisis. The notion that the CCP would make it to fifty seemed doubtful. Still less likely was a sixtieth birthday – an especially resonant turning point, given Chinese traditions of timekeeping. The lunar calendar is based on the twelve signs of the zodiac being paired in succession with the five elements, meaning that completing a sixty year cycle is symbolically a bit like completing a century in standard Western timekeeping traditions. Nor would the 2009 birthday spectacle that Hu presided over be some kind of last hurrah. It would be followed in September 2015 by the grand military pageant that his successor, Xi, organised, ostensibly to mark the seventieth anniversary of the Japanese surrender at the close of World War II, but actually to showcase the might of the People's Liberation Army, the military arm of the CCP. Now, in 2016, Beijing is heading into a five-year countdown to the moment in 2021 when, unless something unexpected happens, the country will mark the centenary of the Party's founding.

What turned the tides, extending so dramatically the life course of an organisation that seemed to be on its deathbed? It's impossible to pinpoint when exactly the CCP went from looking like it was on its last legs to looming as a global *force majeure*. But as curious as it sounds, the mistaken predictions of my generation may have helped bring about its rise – and the events in Berlin.

I was enlightened in 1999 at a Budapest conference devoted to revisiting the end of the wall one decade on. After a presentation by a group of American print and broadcast journalists, including *New York Times* writers Flora Lewis and R.W. Apple Jr., Central European University historian István Rév made a comment that, to him, may have been simply an off-the-cuff remark, but to many of us was stunningly profound. The journalists had expressed pride in how they had described and analysed breaking news events ten years earlier. But they lamented their failure to predict sooner the dramatic changes these protests would yield. They failed to foresee that the marches and rallies were not just newsworthy – they were of great historical consequence.

Rév, however, thanked the journalists for their 'failure' to predict that consequence; he and the countless others who had longed for change owed them a debt of gratitude for their lack of clairvoyance. Living under Communist Party rule, he said, taught people that taking actions deemed to be of 'world historical importance' would end in bloodshed. In essence, if the world had believed that the wall would come down, many ordinary citizens in communist-run parts of Europe would have stayed home, fearing that the governments of the Iron Curtain would act forcefully to crush their protests. What happened instead was that the world's disbelief in radical change emboldened the participants in the European upheaval of 1989. Ironically, the perceived futility of the marches helped make that year's miracles possible.

That conference in Budapest, which I thought about a lot as the sixtieth anniversary of the PRC's founding was being marked, led me to a different but complementary conclusion about prediction as it related to China. Namely, one reason the CCP had endured was that, in the wake of the fall of the Berlin Wall and the 1991 implosion of the Soviet Union, its demise had seemed so inevitable.

China, unlike the Eastern European states, had early warning that its regime was about to fall; the entire world seemed to know it. That sense of urgency made Chinese leaders, from Deng Xiaoping on, avid students of the Soviet Union's downfall, setting a trend that has continued into the current era of Xi Jinping. The CCP charged official think tanks with discovering the keys to maintaining a monopoly on power, while avoiding the fate of erstwhile counterparts in Budapest, Bucharest, Moscow, and Prague.

What did the Chinese researchers learn? First, that Europe's 1989 unrest was fuelled by patriotism – a desire to rid their countries of regimes imposed from outside. Protesters in Europe also had a potent mix of economic and political grievances. Those in charge had claimed that Marxist regimes could compete with capitalist ones in material terms, but the night-and-day contrast between the creature comforts available on the two sides of the wall revealed the hollowness of this boast. Finally, Eastern Europe's movements spread quickly because nearly everyone – regardless of their class – felt that they were in the same boat. The only meaningful social divide was between a small privileged coterie of corrupt officials and the rest. And the rest was pretty much everyone.

It should be no surprise, then, that CCP leaders took steps to counter each of these lessons throughout the 1990s. They placed renewed emphasis on patriotic education, stressing the party's pre-1949 role in chasing out foreign invaders. As an antidote to a widespread sense of economic privation, a consumer revolution began, minimising the contrast between the lifestyles enjoyed by the relatively well-off residents in booming mainland cities and their counterparts in capitalist Taiwan. Perhaps most importantly, China made itself less susceptible to the 'Polish disease', a term for the cross-class mobilisation associated with the Solidarity movement, coined originally in East Germany and eventually made popular in Beijing policy circles. The CCP oversaw an economic boom that created an urban social landscape far more diverse than that of dissident Poland – and that of China itself when the Tiananmen protests won broad sympathy in 1989.

Of course many other factors, including the actions of key individuals such as Mikhail Gorbachev in the Berlin Wall case and Deng in Tiananmen and its aftermath, need to be taken into account to fully explain history unfolding as it did. Still, as the 2009 anniversaries came and went, the irony of prediction was well worth remembering. One reason the Berlin Wall fell was because it once seemed so likely to endure. And one reason the CCP endured to celebrate sixty years in power was that it once seemed so likely to fall, and as a result made shrewd diagnostic efforts to avoid suffering that predicted fate. The CCP continues to refine its policies with an eye toward altering the mix of factors that led to massive protests at home and the collapse of kindred regimes abroad in 1989. This ongoing tinkering, informed by what happened in the past, helps account for the Party now having leaders who are gearing up to celebrate the organisation's 100th anniversary in 2021, and who insist that the Party will still be in control in 2049 when China will allegedly realise Xi Jinping's 'Chinese Dream' of a strong and globally admired country.

# III

# Orwell and Huxley

*Who, we sometimes ask, at the dinners and debates of the intelligentsia, was the 20th century's more insightful prophet – Aldous Huxley or George Orwell? Each is best known for his dystopian fantasy – Huxley's Brave New World, Orwell's Nineteen Eighty-Four – and both feared where modern technology might lead, for authorities and individuals alike. But while Huxley anticipated a world of empty pleasures and excessive convenience, Orwell predicted ubiquitous surveillance and the eradication of freedom. Who was right?*

– William Davies, *New Statesman*,
1 August 2005[6]

The long-standing Huxley vs. Orwell debate got a twenty-first century New Media makeover in 2009, courtesy of cartoonist Stuart McMillen. In May of that year, he published an online comic entitled 'Amusing Ourselves to Death' that quickly went viral. At the top of this strip, which has been tweeted and re-tweeted many times and can now be found on scores of websites, we see caricatures of the two authors above their names and the respective titles of their best-known novels. Below that comes a series of couplet-like contrastive statements, accompanied by illustrations. The top couplet reads: 'What Orwell feared were those who would ban books; What Huxley feared was that there would be no need to ban a book, for there would be no one who would want to read one.' The first statement is paired with a picture of a censorship committee behind a desk, with a one-man 'Internet Filter Department' off to one side and a wastebasket for banned books to the other. The illustration for the second statement shows a family of couch potatoes waiting for 'The Biggest Loser' to return after a word from its sponsors.[7]

McMillen's 'Amusing Ourselves to Death' might best be called an homage, or perhaps a reboot, for the lines in it all come straight from media theorist Neil Postman's influential 1985 book of the same title, which made the case for Huxley's famous 1932 novel being a superior guide to the era of television than Orwell's from 1949. But Postman himself was far from the first to play the Huxley vs. Orwell game. The tradition of comparing and contrasting Huxley and Orwell goes back to, well,

Huxley and Orwell, two writers who (though this is not mentioned as often as one might expect) knew one another from Eton, where Orwell, known then solely by his birth name Eric Blair, was Huxley's pupil in the 1910s.

Orwell had not yet written *Nineteen Eighty-Four* when he first questioned his former teacher's prescience. In the early 1940s, a reader of his newspaper column solicited Orwell's opinion of the danger that consumerism and the pursuit of pleasure posed to society. Orwell replied that, in his view, the time to worry about *Brave New World* scenarios had passed, for the danger of a 'completely materialist vulgar civilisation based on hedonism' emerging was no longer the great threat it once had been.[8]

In October 1949, just a few months after Orwell published *Nineteen Eighty-Four* (a work that presumably spelled out the more pressing threats he had in mind), Huxley wrote to his former pupil to make the opposite point. Orwell's book impressed him, he said, but he did not find it completely convincing, because he continued to think, as he had when crafting *Brave New World*, that the elites of the future would find 'less arduous' strategies for satisfying their 'lust for power' than the 'boot-on-the-face' technique described in *Nineteen Eighty-Four*.[9]

Huxley wrote that letter in Britain during a month

that began with a momentous event at the opposite end of Eurasia: the founding of the People's Republic of China. The author did not mention this to Orwell, nor indeed did he bring up any specific country to illustrate his claim. Rather, he contented himself with ruminating in a general way about the contrast between what we now sometimes describe as the divide between 'hard' authoritarianism (the kind associated with, say, present-day North Korea) and 'soft' authoritarianism (for which present-day Singapore, which science fiction author William Gibson memorably described in *Wired* as 'Disneyland with the Death Penalty'[10], is often considered the poster child).

Over time, though, the PRC would start to be brought into the Huxley-Orwell debate quite regularly, nearly always to make the point that *Nineteen Eighty-Four* was a more prophetic text than *Brave New World*. This is hardly surprising, given that Orwell's book is usually taken as an allegory of Stalinist communism, and the PRC was founded, and still is run, by a Communist Party. For though Orwell was a fierce critic of imperialism and fascism as well as state socialism (and actually claimed to draw inspiration for some aspects of *Nineteen Eighty-Four* from his time working for the BBC), soon after the start of the Mao era (1949–76) it became an article of faith for critics of communism that countries run by Leninist parties were quintessential 'Big Brother' states.

The idea that Orwell rather than Huxley was the one to turn to if one wanted a fictional lens through which to peer at China went virtually unchallenged throughout the Cold War – except, it is worth noting, by Huxley himself. In *Brave New World Revisited*, published in 1958, he argued that Mao had created a system that synthesised elements of *Brave New World* and *Nineteen Eighty-Four*. Most foreign analysts would have none of this. They took it for granted that Communist Party leaders, including those in Beijing, offered the classic example of rulers who made everyone accept (or at least pretend to accept) that 2 + 2 = 5. And dissidents in various communist countries who managed to lay their hands on forbidden editions of *Nineteen Eighty-Four* generally agreed with this assessment.

In this regard, things had not changed all that much by 2010. The prologue to Charles Horner's *Rising China and Its Postmodern Fate* (2009), for example, evoked this Cold War common sense about the PRC. Looking back to his school years, Horner, who would go on to become a long-time student of PRC politics, claimed that 'actually existing China' (as opposed to the mythic pre-1949 locale conjured up in Pearl Buck novels and stories told by widely travelled family members) 'first appeared to me in an English class, where we read George Orwell's *Nineteen Eighty-Four*'. He recounts a teacher showing members of his class a 'long article that had appeared in *Newsweek* describing a vast, government-engineered upheaval in China called the Great Leap Forward'. In this magazine piece, according to Horner, 'Chairman Mao's campaign was described . . . as an ur-nightmare of totalitarianism, right down to his naming of it with a perfectly Orwellian phrase.'[11]

*Nineteen Eighty-Four* remains a common reference point in discussions of contemporary China – though it is fair to say that, in the wake of such developments as Edward Snowden's leak of NSA surveillance activities and reports on the proliferation of closed circuit television cameras across the United Kingdom, there is more and more talk of Western democracies having Big Brother state-like dimensions as well. The tendency to view the PRC as above all a *Nineteen Eighty-Four* state has continued, even as it has become – as Cold War era Soviet bloc countries never were, except right before their communist rule ended – a place where translations of that book can be purchased openly, and where dramatisations of Orwell's shorter fictional critique of totalitarianism, *Animal Farm*, can be staged. The clearest sign of the continued hold of the PRC-as-Big-Brother-state line of thinking is what happens annually when the anniversary of the June Fourth massacre arrives. The international press can always be counted on to bring up Orwell, and no wonder, since Beijing's denial that soldiers killed large numbers of civilians in 1989 is a classic illustration of the '2 + 2 = 5' style of Newspeak he parodied. (It was very fitting that Louisa Lim's 2014 book *The People's Republic of Amnesia*, which explores this issue, was shortlisted for, among other awards, the 2015 Orwell Prize.)

The adjective 'Orwellian' is used regularly in stories about Beijing's efforts to control the kinds of information people can access online and monitor what people do in internet cafés. Allusions to *Nineteen Eighty-Four* also appear often when the authorities get tough with dissenters. In 2011, for example, when the Chinese authorities – made skittish no doubt by the spectre of events in the Middle East – launched a crackdown on political gadfly figures, this was described as a turn toward Big Brother modes of control. And in that same year, a contributor to the *Guardian* called the April 2011 arrest of iconoclastic artist Ai Weiwei a reminder that Chinese dissidents can still find themselves 'blackguarded and bullied with total impunity by a system that takes Orwell's *1984* as a handbook'.[12]

The continued allure of *Nineteen Eighty-Four* analogies to describe contemporary China has also been underscored in coverage of two specific twenty-first century topics: the very large number of state-controlled video cameras that keep tabs on China's public spaces (these are sometimes said in the Western press to 'raise the specter of genuinely Orwellian control'[13]) and the publication first in Chinese language editions in Hong Kong and Taiwan, and then in English translation as *The Fat Years*, of Chan Koonchung's *Shengshi Zhongguo 2013*, a dystopian novel set in the PRC in the eponymous year, which has now passed but still lay in the near future when the work was written. Chan's novel, which has never been published on the mainland, was dubbed a 'Chinese *Nineteen Eighty-Four*' in many reports. This was partly due to its title containing the name of a year, but mostly due to its portrayal of a tightly controlled China of the future, in which a recent outburst of protest has been expunged from the minds of Chinese citizens.

Even though ruminations on China's Orwellian features have not gone away, a countervailing trend toward looking at the PRC through the lens provided by *Brave New World* has recently gained steam – and it is worth noting that Chan's novel makes no mention of Orwell but does give a shout out to Huxley. I first became interested in *Brave New World's* relevance to China in 2003, when asked to give a talk about the June Fourth massacre to a group of college freshmen who had all just read Huxley's famous novel. I've returned to the subject several times since, exploring from different angles the question of whether the PRC is best seen as a 'Big Brother' state of 'boot-on-the-face' forms of repression, a country of 'vulgar materialism' like the one Huxley imagined, or a mash-up of the two.

In wrestling with this issue, I've drawn attention to several things. One is the contrast between Orwell's focus on the way governments *watch people* and Huxley's emphasis on how order is maintained in part by the things that *people watch*.

Another area I stress is that, while Communist Party leaders have tended to take a dim view of novels skewering authoritarian systems and often made sale of them illegal, both *Nineteen Eighty-Four*, which is well known to Chinese readers, and *Brave New World*, which is less famous in the PRC, are readily available for sale across the mainland. They are even available in a three-volume dystopian classics boxed set, which also includes *Animal Farm* (bundled together with *Nineteen Eighty-Four*), *Brave New World* (printed as a single volume with *Brave New World Revisited*), and Yevgeny Zamyatin's *We*, a 1921 work that influenced both Orwell and Huxley. The fact that these and other formerly banned works are now openly sold could be read as a sign that the CCP of today is more self-confident about its hold on power than it was in the past, especially in comparison to past Leninist regimes whose leaders banned such works. It may also reflect the government's current interest in providing consumers, including intellectuals and others drawn toward books of these kinds, with the sorts of things they like to buy. (One key thing, though, is missing from the dystopian trilogy: a translation of the specific passages of *Brave New World Revisited* that refer to the dark side of life in post-1949 China.)

A third aspect I have emphasised in some past writings is the need to keep in mind that different modes of control predominate in different sections of the PRC. The 'hard authoritarianism' Orwell imagined is often the rule in frontier zones such as Tibet and Xinjiang, just as it is in North Korea. In the booming cities of China's eastern seaboard, however, the 'soft authoritarianism' of *Brave New World*, which brings to mind Singapore more than Pyongyang, is frequently the order of the day, except at particularly sensitive moments, when Orwellian patterns come to the fore. In Hong Kong, there is an even more pronounced tilt in the *Brave New World* direction – one reason that the 'boot-on-the-face' Orwellian use of tear gas against protesters during the Umbrella Movement had such a galvanising effect on the local populace.

One time that the Orwell-Huxley issue was at the front of my mind was during late June and July of 2010, a period I spent in Shanghai, the best known and most spectacle-driven of Chinese boomtowns. At the time, the city was mid-way through hosting the 2010 World Expo, the most expensive, largest and most visited planned event in human history. It was also, alas, the World's Fair with the longest lines (more than three hours for the most popular national pavilions) and surely some of the worst weather (with record-breaking high temperatures recorded on a massive thermometer, of record-breaking height, made out of an old factory smokestack). Since *Brave New World* is a novel that has much to say about high-tech forms of entertainment (such as the pornographic 'feelies' that help keep denizens of that dystopia distracted), the 2010 World Expo with its many (admittedly family friendly) state-of-the-art cinematic works seemed at first custom-made for an analysis that drew heavily on Huxley. However, my stay in Shanghai also coincided with reports of stepped up surveillance methods in Xinjiang, as the first anniversary of the 2009 riots there came and went. Reading stories about what was happening in that northwestern region brought Orwell to mind.

It might seem from this précis that my 2010 stay in China would have simply confirmed my previous sense of the PRC being divided up into Orwell and Huxley zones. But things are not so simple, and elements of the two writers' duelling dystopias often co-exist in the same space. The Shanghai Expo was just such a space. The *Brave New World* aspects of the World's Fair genre, and the Disney theme parks that should be seen as part of the same lineage of spectacle, are obvious enough: these mega-events, from the 1851 fair held in London's Crystal Palace onwards, have always been largely about two things. One is consumption – this is why cultural critic Walter Benjamin famously referred to them as sites of 'pilgrimage to the commodity fetish'. The other is escapist entertainment. The first Ferris Wheel was a hit at the 1893 Chicago Columbian Exposition, as were performances by Buffalo Bill's Wild West Show and other companies known for dramatic re-enactments of historical and legendary events. The Shanghai Expo was not lacking in either of these features (nor was the far less grandiose 2015 sequel in Milan, which I visited as well).

In addition, in line with *Brave New World*'s focus on pleasure rather than fear, World's Fair and World Expo displays tend to be as upbeat as the rose-coloured view of simpler times on Main Street, and the high-tech futuristic Tomorrowland exhibitions at Disneyland. They typically stress the growing comforts of modern life and the prospect of a better world to come. When looking backward, they do so only with nostalgia and a focus on how the past has prepared us to live better lives now. Their exhibits typically contain few mentions of the anxieties of war and concern with enemies that Orwell imagined being a central part of our future. True, early World's Fairs often displayed state-of-the-art military hardware (one of the longest lines in Chicago in 1893 was to see a massive piece of artillery) and featured parades by soldiers wearing the uniforms of different nations and empires (a notable attraction at the Paris Universal Exposition of 1900). In addition, a famous work of art showing war's devastation (Picasso's 'Guernica') made its debut at the World of Tomorrow Exposition held in New York in 1939. Nevertheless, the overall thrust of these events has generally been (and remains) to accentuate the positive.

The specific focus of the Shanghai Expo, held in a city whose massive Disneyland Park is scheduled to open in 2016, was the challenge to the world posed by rapid urbanisation. This does not, however, mean that the displays lingered on dark environmental issues – nor were famine and food scares a central concern at the edibles-oriented Milan Expo. Rather, the 2010 Expo's mission was to draw attention to how much people working together toward common goals could do to solve urban problems. International cooperation was celebrated just as resolutely at the Shanghai Expo as it was in the 'It's a Small World' ride (a simulated tour of the planet via slow-moving boats, which pass by dancing and singing mechanical puppets dressed to evoke different locales), which Walt Disney designed for New York's 1964/65 World's Fair, a ride that went on to serve as an emblematic attraction at all Disney theme parks.

There was an optimistic feel to most of the nearly 200 national pavilions that were the main attraction of the Pudong (East Shanghai) side of the 2010 fairgrounds, which gave the setting an 'Epcot-on-steroids' feel. The same went for most of the pavilions across the river in Puxi (West Shanghai). These were devoted not to nations but to corporations (GM had one), cities (the Liverpool pavilion, in which the Beatles made a virtual cameo, was a great crowd pleaser), and such topics as imagining the urban future.

The exhibits in all of these pavilions were designed to be distracting and immersive, like *Brave New World*'s erotic 'feelies', sans the sexuality. Some of the exhibits had elements that were interactive (you could ride a chair lift in the Swiss Pavilion, for instance, and get a panoramic view of a faux Europe made up of nearby national pavilions when it reached its greatest height), but most were designed for passive viewing (many countries, including the United States, relied heavily upon films to tell the story of their nations). Nearly all displays downplayed explicitly political subjects, and history was generally brought into the picture, as it was in a special pavilion devoted to the history of World's Fairs and World Expos, in a tidy fashion—always as great things that happened in the past that had paved the way for even better things to come.

All this may seem far removed from *Nineteen Eighty-Four,* but there were many specific points during my visit when Orwell's novel came to mind. One of the most significant things about any World's Fair is that it affords visitors the opportunity to make imaginary forays to places they may never see in person. That (and the fact that lines to enter them were so short) made stopping in at the Iranian, Cuban, and North Korean pavilions a must for me. At the last of these I found, not surprisingly, a rosy presentation of the land of Kim Jong-Il. In her justly-acclaimed *Nothing to Envy: Ordinary Lives in North Korea*, which makes creative and effective use of interviews with North Korean defectors, Barbara Demick portrays the country as a starkly Orwellian place. Late in the book she mentions that one of her interviewees, upon reading *Nineteen Eighty-Four* after relocating to Seoul, 'marveled that George Orwell could have so understood the North Korean brand of totalitarianism'.[14]

The virtual North Korea that I entered at the fairground, by contrast, was anything but dystopian, filled as it was with video loops of well-fed people (no evidence of the famine Demick and others have detailed) and skies with rainbows. This simulation of North Korean life (artificial even by Expo or Disneyland standards) failed to convince me that Kim Il-Sung and his successors have created a 'people's paradise' (a term used in the exhibit). Still, watching the videos there did make me wonder whether I have been too hasty to embrace the idea that only Orwell has relevance; one piece of footage in particular jumped out at me, for it showed an amusement park, suggesting that even in generally Orwellian

North Korea, a 'less arduous' bread-and-circuses approach can sometimes play a role in subduing the population (at least a very privileged segment of it).

The strongest sense of Big Brother's presence I felt while at the Shanghai Expo – and this had no parallel when I visited the Milan Expo five years later – came after I had left the North Korean exhibit. Walking toward my next stop in the Pudong section of the Expo, I got a text message on my cell phone (a Chinese one linked to China Mobile, one of the country's three intertwined mobile service providers), which listed some shows that would be starting soon in pavilions near me. Later that day, when I crossed the river, a new message came, which informed me that, now that I was in Puxi, I should know about the special events taking place in that part of the fairground. It's fine to see a contrast between Huxley's focus on what we watch and Orwell's on who watches us, but as these unbidden texts reminded me, Big Brother can make his presence known in many ways, by giving entertainment advice as well as by issuing warnings. (Mass text messaging is sometimes used by the Chinese state to convey darker messages; initially tolerated nationalistic protesters have sometimes been told by China Mobile that the government's patience with them is getting strained, so they would do well to get off the streets unless they want to take the chance of being arrested.)

A final Orwellian experience I had at the Expo reminded me that there are many ways for inconvenient bits of history to be airbrushed away. When I went to the pavilion devoted to past World's Fairs and Expos, I was especially interested to see how one exhibition in particular was dealt with: the 1964/65 fair held in Flushing, New York, which had provided me with my only previous World's Fair experience. Inside the pavilion there were visual reminders of many other World's Fairs (I walked beneath a mock Eiffel Tower, saw posters featuring Seattle's Space Needle, read about the ice cream cone being invented in St. Louis in 1904, and so on), but I came across no mention or visual allusion to the one I had gone to as a tot. Why? Because the 1964/65 World's Fair was not officially recognised by the Bureau International des Expositions, the official body that is to World Expos what the IOC is to the Olympics. It was held too soon after another American event, the Seattle World Expo, for the BIE's liking. Due to this, and the fact that Cold War politics meant only a smattering of countries participated in it, New York's last fair is sometimes seen as separate from the Expo lineage.

I'm not sure what role, if any, the BIE played in ensuring that I'd see no evidence of the one World's Fair I remembered while at the 2010 Expo. It would certainly not surprise me to learn that the Chinese organisers were asked to keep their officially recognised

Expo free of all reminders of that earlier unofficial one, and complied happily. For there would be no novelty for them about pretending that a famous event had never happened.

# IV

# China and Russia

Once upon a time, specialists in Chinese studies felt a kinship with scholars who focused on Russia. We each shared an interest in large countries that had command economies and Leninist systems of rule. We each struggled to make sense of comparably opaque and often misleading official pronouncements. But then came an event whose twentieth anniversary was marked in 2011: the collapse of the Soviet Union. In the wake of this great change, the comparative landscape began to shift. Soon, the contrasts between China and Russia seemed to far outweigh their similarities. After all, as 1991 ended, new leaders in Moscow were preparing to leave the communist era behind, while their counterparts in Beijing were expressing determination to keep China under Communist Party control and territorially intact.

And yet, some twenty years after the alleged parting of the ways between Moscow and Beijing, something strange began to happen when I read stories about Russia with the goal, in part, of briefly forgetting about China. My effort to escape would be undermined by a feeling that the words coming off the page could just as well have been written about the country I teach and write about for a living. This has been occurring more and more frequently of late.

One of the first times I had this sensation was while reading *New Yorker* editor David Remnick's fascinating 'Letter from Moscow: The Civil Archipelago', which appeared in his magazine's final issue of 2011. Focusing largely on responses to Russia's late 2011 elections, it offered a sweeping look at everything from the complex and challenging activities of human rights groups, to the underdeveloped nature of civil society in a post-totalitarian state, to the limits placed on the press in a country whose leaders were determined to contain the flow of any information that undermined their authority. The big themes Remnick addressed often brought Chinese examples to my mind, but so, too, did some of the essay's small details. For example, in trying to capture the frustration and outrage that many urban residents felt at the special perks enjoyed by members and friends of the government, Remnick turned to driving habits. Solving traffic congestion in Moscow was a simple matter for 'officials and the well-connected', who employed specially issued 'flashing blue lights' that, when placed atop their luxury cars, allowed them to zoom through traffic-snarled streets as ordinary drivers had to pull aside to let them pass.[15] To be sure, China has never had the same blue light system. Nevertheless, the Chinese Internet circa 2011 was filled with angry posts describing incidents when officials and their family members acted – and got away with acting – as though the rules did not apply to them. And, to be sure, China also had traffic-related perks for officials and drivers of military vehicles.

I felt a particularly strong sense of 'he could have just come back from China' as Remnick described a spate of urban protests in Russia. For Remnick, this form of resistance demonstrated that the authoritarian country's young professionals were becoming less 'bovine', 'apathetic', and 'anesthetized by stability' than they once were. This assessment of Russia's middle class struck me as something I could have just as easily read on the 'Letter from China' blog that *New Yorker* staffer Evan Osnos was keeping in 2011. It is not just that Osnos, like other China-based journalists, pointed to the same sort of increases in middle class restiveness and sometimes activism that caught Remnick's attention. It was also that, as Osnos often pointed out in his blog and would later stress in his 2014 book, *Age of Ambition*, the Chinese authorities had been working overtime to convince upwardly mobile young professionals to continue to accept a flawed status quo, as long as it brought them creature comforts – a deal that the government struck with this demographic group in the wake of 1989, and one that seemed to be less and less secure as time went by.[16]

One particular Osnos post on this theme, written a year before Remnick's 'The Civil Archipelago' essay, was called 'The Age of Complacency?' Its focus was Chan's dystopian novel, *The Fat Years*, which examined, according to Osnos, how 'the most privileged and educated men and women' in a China just over the horizon 'struggle to balance the benefits and perils of life under high-functioning authoritarianism'.[17] The novel encouraged us to reflect, Osnos claimed, on the choices that lay before those who, as opposed to being left behind during their country's rise, had 'reaped the rewards' of economic development, but had begun to wonder if in the process they had sacrificed too much in the way of political liberties. Remnick identified a similarly tricky situation in Russia, at a time when there was increasing unease with Putin's government among not just dissidents and the poor, but also some who had been doing quite well for themselves in recent years.

When *Age of Ambition* arrived, it was filled with additional material that spoke to the themes of Remnick's essay, including chapters on government moves to intimidate or silence nuisance figures, such as the globally famous Ai Weiwei and many less internationally famous figures. Some of these moves to quell freedom of expression were launched in 2011, in part because Beijing was jumping at shadows in the wake of the Arab Spring, worried that Hosni Mubarak's fall in Egypt might presage their own demise at the hands of an angry populace. And, as Remnick noted, the same was true for Russia at that time. The swift transformations in the Middle East and North Africa in early 2011 ensured that the year would be a nervous one for authoritarian leaders of all ideological persuasions, and Remnick's depiction of the anxiety in Russian leadership circles was eerily similar in tone to those nervous shudders emanating from Beijing.

The tense state of affairs in Chechnya, a frontier zone with a largely Muslim population, did nothing to assuage fears of actual resistance spreading to the capital. Remnick's 'The Civil Archipelago' highlighted these regional 'differences' within Russia. He wrote that authorities were particularly 'ruthless' and 'draconian' in dealing with any hint of dissent there, and described the dangers journalists face in reporting on and from the region. Chechnya lingered as perhaps the biggest failure of 'democratic' Russia, making that post-communist country not so different, again, from its still-communist neighbour.

China's closest counterpart to Chechnya, which is at the very edge of the Russian Federation, was and still remains Xinjiang, a similarly distant outpost of the PRC. In a July 2009 'Letter from China' post called 'Looking Beyond Ethnicity', Osnos referred to Beijing's 'decades of trying, unsuccessfully, to snuff out resistance' in Xinjiang. The Party's mishandling of Uyghur-Han tensions had resulted in a region 'embroiled in a pattern of uprising and crackdown' that contrasted sharply with the situation in most other parts of the country. In a follow-up ('Xinjiang: The Reckoning Begins'), Osnos described a Han man armed with a stick who tore open a car door to threaten the pair of foreign reporters inside.[18]

The similarities between Russia and China should not be overstated. National elections, no matter how flawed, have been held in recent decades in the former but not the latter. Chechnya is not just like Xinjiang. Putin circa 2011, already a man known for grand gestures and dramatic posturing, was very different from his pallid Chinese counterpart, Hu Jintao.

Still, even though any China-Russia analogy is bound to be imperfect, imperfect analogies can be useful. They can lead us to break out of entrenched, misleading modes of thinking, help us become attentive to connections and parallels we might otherwise miss, and, in this case, could have prepared us for the growing political ties between Moscow and Beijing. Putting Russia and China in a shared category, rather than one in a post-communist box and the other in a still-communist one, makes it less surprising to hear that leaders in Moscow and Beijing may once more be looking to one other for inspiration about how to handle specific problems. Remnick's one comment about China was, in fact, a reference to members of Putin's circle studying the sophisticated techniques that Chinese authorities have developed in their struggle to control the online flow of dissenting opinions.

The imperfect China-Russia analogy inspires a fanciful thought, triggered in part by two anniversaries in the year 2012: the twentieth anniversary of the founding of the post-Soviet Union state of the Russian Federation and the fortieth of Nixon's historic meeting with Mao Zedong. If a Rip van Winkle figure, prone to two-decade-long naps, woke in late February 1972 after falling asleep in 1952, he would have been shocked to learn that a summit was underway in China between Mao (one of the world's leading communists) and Richard Nixon (a fervently anti-communist American president). But if the same fellow dozed off again in 1992 and woke up in 2012, he would also have been in for an unsettling surprise: that it was no longer easy to tell, without paying close attention to details, whether a *New Yorker* 'Letter from . . .' commentary was about a post-communist Moscow or the still-communist Beijing.

Here, though, is a still more interesting Rip van Winkle exercise to ponder: what if someone tracking relations between Moscow and Beijing had gone to sleep in 1965 and awoken in 2015 in time to watch the grand victory parades, marking World War II anniversaries, staged in the two capitals. In 1965, communist leaders were in charge in both Moscow and Beijing, but they were at odds with one another. How bizarre, then, for our Rip van Winkle to discover in 2015 that the most powerful foreign guest to attend Moscow's celebration of the seventieth anniversary of Germany's defeat was the Chinese communist leader Xi Jinping – and that the most powerful foreign guest on the rostrum, as missiles rolled by Tiananmen Square to mark the seventieth anniversary of Japan's surrender, was Putin.

# V

# Yu Hua and Mark Twain

What if Yu Hua had become the first Chinese author, still based in China, to win a Nobel Prize for Literature?

Was Mark Twain a dissident?

I've been pondering this pair of questions about two of my favourite authors since the news broke in November 2012 that Mo Yan had been elevated to the status of literary laureate. This immediately sparked a passionate debate on the pros and cons of the Nobel committee's choice, to which not only specialists in Chinese literature but also figures like Salman Rushdie and Pankaj Mishra, contributed.

One camp was angered by the committee's choice. These commentators, Rushdie among them, decried the award going to a man they saw as a loyal servant of a vile authoritarian state.[19] This group cited the new laureate's role as co-chairman of the official Writers Association as 'proof' that Mo Yan (a pen name;

he was born Guan Moye) was a government stooge, and thus by definition a bad choice for the award.

A second camp argued that, to the contrary, Mo Yan was a worthy recipient of the honour. They saw him as talented and also 'subtly' but 'profoundly subversive', as literary scholar Sabina Knight put it in an essay for the *National Interest*.[20]

Some of Mo Yan's books have run afoul of the state's censorship system, she stresses, and it is unfair to make him 'a scapegoat for the sins of the regime in which he must survive'. Such defenders of the Nobel nod draw attention to the author's portrayals of the hardships of ordinary people and his satirising of corrupt local officials. Mo Yan challenges the political status quo, Knight insists, through his magical realism and his heroes' 'almost-libertarian allegiance to personal freedom'.

There are still others, including Mishra, who have steered clear of both damning the Nobel selectors and celebrating the Chinese author, preferring to muse instead on a political litmus test. Mishra and company emphasise that it is only when the author in question is from Western Europe or North America that we tend to focus largely or exclusively on the quality of a laureate's writings, rather than on whether he or she has subservient or subversive leanings.[21]

Members of this third camp could have buttressed their case by bringing up Mark Twain. He never won a

Nobel, but had he received one during the short period when he was alive and they were being handed out, he *could* have been presented as an establishment writer who counted presidents among his friends. He could also, though, have been presented as an anti-establishment firebrand whose criticisms of imperialism, as Selina Lai-Henderson notes in her fascinating new book, *Mark Twain in China*, led one newspaper to describe him as the United States' 'most dreaded critic of the sacrosanct person in the White House'. [22] And yet, because he was American and was not seen as working within an authoritarian setting, it seems unlikely that there would have been a debate over whether he was best seen as a subversive or a stooge.

If, however, the 2012 Nobel had gone not to Mo Yan but to Yu Hua, a Chinese writer I have come to think of as having many things in common with Twain, this very likely *would* have occurred. Politically, Yu Hua is a much more daring figure than Mo Yan, but he, too, is neither a dissident nor a sell-out. Yet, had he won, the same kinds of moves to brand him as one or the other that took place with the actual winner in November 2012 would surely have been made.

I was likely the only one to think of both Mark Twain and Yu Hua when Mo Yan won his prize, due largely to the fact that both have come to occupy similar places in my personal pantheon of exalted literary figures.

My appreciation for Twain goes back to my reading him as a teenager in the 1970s, though I knew his name and those of many of his characters even earlier, thanks to a childhood that included exposure to television shows and films based on novels such as *Adventures of Huckleberry Finn*, as well as visits to Disneyland that were never complete without a stop at Tom Sawyer's Island. It took a college class devoted to the author, though, to transform me from a casual enthusiast to an ardent fan.

Prior to taking the class, I thought of Twain as a skilful author of humorous novels. He is, of course, much more than that. He wrote great parables, such as his career-launching one about a jumping frog; memoirs, such as *Life on the Mississippi*, which is also a history of steamboat piloting before the Civil War; books that present embellished versions of real life travels, such as *The Innocents Abroad*, which remained his best-selling book throughout his lifetime; and trenchant essays, such as 'To the Person Sitting in Darkness', a powerful condemnation of the often barbaric side of Western efforts to bring 'civilisation' to other parts of the world. Ever since taking that course more than three decades ago, if asked to name my favourite American author, I've had a ready answer: the man born Samuel Clemens.

The Chinese writer I paid most attention to in college was not Yu Hua, who hadn't yet begun to publish, but

Lu Xun (1881–1936). For many years, if asked to name my favourite Chinese author, I would say the name of this figure who, as I learned from Lai-Henderson's book, greatly admired the way that Huck Finn's creator 'imbued humor with bitterness and sarcasm' in his writings. Lu Xun (born Zhou Shuren) is best known for his short stories, including 'Diary of a Madman', a searing and surreal indictment of Confucianism, and the darkly comic novella *The True Story of Ah Q*. He also wrote compelling essays about politics, language, folklore, and many other topics. When, in the 1980s and 1990s, I told people who were from China or familiar with the country that Lu Xun was my favourite Chinese writer, they would simply nod, as if it were expected, which in fact it likely was. He is, after all, widely viewed as the country's most significant modern literary figure.

My discovery of Yu came later, well after this onetime dentist, who first made his mark with surrealistic short stories published in the mid-1980s, had become known. By the time I began to read him, he had two late twentieth-century novels under his belt that had each earned critical raves. The first of these, *To Live*, was made into a movie by Zhang Yimou, while the second, *Chronicle of a Blood Merchant*, was hailed by many as one of the best novels published in China in the 1990s.

Still not a household name in the West, Yu has recently become better known to Anglophone readers, thanks to four books coming out in translation in the early years of the twenty-first century. These are *Brothers*, a sprawling novel set largely during the Cultural Revolution; *China in Ten Words*, a work of nonfiction; the short story collection *Boy in the Twilight* (which appeared in Chinese in 1999 but not in English until 2014); and the novella *The Seventh Day* (the English language edition of which was published in 2015). Adding further to Yu's international reputation have been the often wickedly funny, sometimes moving, and always insightful commentaries on contemporary issues, from censorship and historical commemoration to food safety scares and Chinese images of the United States, which he has contributed to publications such as the *New York Times* and Britain's *Prospect* magazine.

I've yet to tackle some of Yu's fictional works, including *Brothers*, which was published in China in 2005 and translated into English by the talented team of Eileen Cheng-yin Chow and Carlos Rojas in 2009, but I have liked all the short stories and novels I've read. I am equally fond of his nonfiction, especially *Ten Words*, Yu's 2012 collection of memoir-infused reflections on key terms, which benefits from a brisk and wonderfully effective translation by Allan H. Barr, who also rendered *Boy in the Twilight* and *Seventh Day* into English. When people ask me to suggest a novel dealing with the rise and rule of China's Communist Party, I point them toward *To Live*, which is available in a lively translation by Michael Berry and presents pivotal stages of revolutionary history from the perspective of everyman characters, or else *Chronicle of a Blood Merchant*, which has similar virtues and a slightly larger quotient of humour. It was translated into English by the talented Andrew F. Jones, who also contributes a thoughtful introduction on Yu's career and style. To those who say they are looking for a highly readable work by a Chinese author that provides an illuminating perspective on the country today, I say they can't do better than *Ten Words*.

As for Lu Xun, whose deep influence on Yu is clear (he even devotes an entire chapter in *Ten Words* to him), I definitely still rate him highly. I continue to be struck by the power of his essays, the emotional wallop of stories like the elegiac 'Hometown', and the way that *The True Story of Ah Q* captures how the 1911 Revolution failed to change fundamental aspects of Chinese society.

When I first realised that Yu was replacing Lu Xun as the Chinese figure whose place in my personal pantheon was most comparable to Twain's, I believed that little beyond that quirk of individual preference linked the old American author to the present-day Chinese one. I had never seen them compared in print or online. Nor had I seen any mention of Yu's thoughts on Twain – though he surely would have come across his work, given the positive reputation the American author has enjoyed in China from the Republican era (1912–49) through the Mao years (1949–76) and beyond. (Lai-Henderson provides interesting details on Chinese translations of Twain, beginning with an obscure short story translated in 1904, and includes quotes praising the author by not only Lu Xun but also Lao She, another towering literary figure who is said to have almost become China's first literary laureate, had the Nobel committee not been confounded on how to contact him in the PRC in the 1960s. She does not mention Yu Hua, however.) Nevertheless, I've now come to believe that Yu and Twain deserve to be seen as kindred spirits.

Consider what a roomful of educated Americans might say when asked to describe Twain. He was a novelist, one might answer; a satirist, a second might chime in; someone who wrote short stories, which often included absurd events, a third person might add.

Those most familiar with Twain's oeuvre – due, for example, to having taken a course on him – might offer more details. They might point out that Twain liked to experiment with styles and genres (*A Connecticut Yankee in King Arthur's Court*, for example, has been classified as a work of science fiction as well as of historical fiction); that he wrote nonfiction books as well as novels, excelling as a pointed, often amusing cultural and political critic; that he often drew heavily on his experiences growing up outside major metropolitan areas during a tumultuous period; and that, as an adult, he lived through and chronicled a 'gilded age' (a term he helped popularise in a co-authored eponymous book), during which the country of his birth rose rapidly in international prominence. In addition, some of his more censorious peers thought his work unsafe for general consumption, and editors and publishers sometimes objected to his handling of hot button issues.

All but one of these attributes also applies to Yu. The sole exception is that Yu has not, at least so far, helped popularise the name of an era. (This could change; the chapter devoted to 'disparity' in *Ten Words* does such a good job of capturing contemporary inequities that one could imagine the phrase 'Age of Disparity' someday gaining traction for this period, which is already sometimes called China's 'Gilded Age'.)

Yu's oeuvre includes not only the books alluded to so far, but also a collection of early short stories, *The Past and the Punishments*, elegantly translated by Andrew F. Jones. In those early tales, we find Yu trying his hand at everything from a martial arts story to surrealist narratives.

Yu has written an impressive body of short works of criticism. Some of these became, in expanded form, chapters in *China in Ten Words*.

In terms of subject matter, in both his nonfiction and fiction, Yu often draws on memories of growing up in a provincial setting during the tumultuous Cultural Revolution era. Some of his most effective writing, both in novels – from the early *To Live* to the recent *The Seventh Day* – and in *China in Ten Words*, focuses on the experiences of boys and young men.

The parallels between the two writers aren't exact, of course, and there are many contrasts between them to note. For example, throughout his career, Twain wrote travel books. Yu, by contrast, has gone to other countries but generally sticks to domestic settings in his writing. And though Yu can be a lively and funny speaker, he does not, as Twain did, earn a significant amount of his money on the lecture circuit.

Another difference relates to censorship. Twain had periodic run-ins with censors, including spats with newspaper editors who objected to his scathing indictment of the treatment of Chinese immigrants, which editors worried might alienate readers from the ethnic groups that he pilloried for holding these unfair prejudices. These incidents did not play as central a part in his writing life as censorship issues do in those of many contemporary Chinese writers, including Yu, who regularly writes things that he knows can't be published on the Chinese mainland, including anything that tackles a taboo topic such as 1989's June Fourth massacre.

Typically, his fiction is approved for publication in all parts of Greater China, while his nonfiction appears only in translation and in Hong Kong and Taiwan as traditional Chinese character editions.

Yet another contrast has to do with sensibility. Twain was deeply pessimistic. Yu, by contrast, despite writing at times about deeply tragic events (in *The Seventh Day*, nearly every character has suffered a tragedy), tends to be more of an optimist, even though his circumstances could easily lead to a sense of total despair. When he was asked during a talk I attended at Pomona College if he was distressed that some of his work couldn't be sold in bookstores in Beijing, the city he calls home, he said he did not like the situation but saw grounds for hope. He noted that even his 'banned' writings make their way into the country via underground channels, and he said that he was sure the day would come when *Ten Words*, still now too hot for Beijing bookstores to handle, would be sold openly in China's capital.

There is a final difference that strikes me as particularly revealing and brings us back to the debate discussed at the start of this chapter. When I mention Yu at public talks, I'm sometimes asked if he's a 'dissident', or to explain why, if he is as edgy a writer as I suggest, he isn't in jail or in exile. This just isn't the sort of question I imagine people posing about Twain in his day; he was careful not to ally himself with political movements. And yet I do see political as well as literary parallels between the two authors.

Twain often spoke out on issues of his day. He tended to champion the interests of the powerless against the powerful and to mock hypocritical actions by elites. He periodically played, long into his life, the role of an aging *enfant terrible*, yet did not set himself in direct opposition to the political order.

Interestingly, Twain's work stayed in favour in Mao's China, mainly because of the gimlet eye he turned on domestic politics in the United States in stories such as 'Running for Governor', whose enduring popularity across the Pacific was addressed by Amy Qin in a 2014 essay for the *New York Times*. Twain of course was a trenchant critic of American imperialism and what he saw as the immoral and unchristian things said and done by many American missionaries. (Had he been born in China, he famously said in 1900, he would have joined the anti-Christian Boxer movement.) [23]

If, by some chance, Yu is awarded a Nobel Prize and his works gain many new Western readers, I believe those suddenly discovering him would split into the 'think of him as a dissident' camp and the 'he's too far from a dissident to deserve acclaim' camp.

Just look, the first group might argue, at how powerfully some chapters in *Ten Words* expose as shams the stories China's current leaders like to tell. They claim to head a party that has always served the 'people', yet in the book's chapter on that term, Yu says the word only began to feel meaningful to him during the uprising of 1989, as a sense of community emerged out of feelings of common purpose generated by the year's protests. In other chapters, the same people might stress, Yu mocks tales told by the government of its alleged commitment to promoting equality.

Critics of this imagined Yu Hua Nobel nod might counter that most of his short stories, including those in *Boy in the Twilight*, lack overt political content. For an author in an authoritarian setting to be taken seriously, some assume, his or her writings need to challenge the system. Yu's collections of short fiction, including *Boy in the Twilight*, though, give us tales of love affairs gone sour, of shifts in the balance of power within couples over time, of a boy's response to being bullied and teased about his dog, and the like.

These detractors might even describe a favourite story of mine from *Boy in the Twilight* as something that should count against rather than for Yu when it comes to assessing his Nobel worthiness. This tale, 'Appendix', is about two brothers who are enthralled by a story their surgeon father tells them about a doctor far from a hospital and all alone who is struck by appendicitis – yet survives by using a mirror and a knife to perform an appendectomy on his own body.

Not long after the brothers hear the story, their father's own appendix grows inflamed and the only ones who are nearby and able to help him get to a hospital are the two boys. Realising that this is the only chance they will ever get to see if their father can live up to the superhero status they had accorded the doctor in the story, they ignore his plea to rush him to the hospital or fetch a doctor and instead go out in search of a mirror and surgical tools. Their father, wracked by pain, begins weeping and implores them to get their mother. They finally do this, and he is rushed to the hospital, where he barely survives a last-minute appendectomy. The tale ends with the narrator, one of the sons, remembering that later in his childhood:

> When we went to bed in the evenings, we would often hear [our father] grumbling to our mother, saying, 'People think that you have given me two sons, but in fact all they are is appendixes. Ordinarily they are of no use whatsoever, and when things are at a critical point they are practically the death of you.'[24]

This story is one that could have been written by a vexed parent in any setting. There is no skewering of the political status quo, overt or veiled, to be found in any of its sentences.

Readers previously unfamiliar with Yu might wonder

whether the same person could have written the politically charged *Ten Words* and the stories in *Boy in the Twilight*. The disjuncture wouldn't seem so strange, however, if they happened to be familiar with Twain's range, with his deftness at switching between genres – alternating between tales of boyhood pranks and penetrating critiques of how those in power make use of the structures they control and how they try to conceal these actions with fancy words. Twain's oeuvre, like Yu's, is filled with works that demonstrate its author's keen eye for the small dramas of everyday life and keen ear for linguistic hypocrisy, though Twain's is rooted in Bible-thumping moralism and American jingoism, while Yu's takes on Chinese Communist Party sophistry. Both, however, relate to the big issues of the time. Twain seemed equally at home, after all, when offering a humorous account of a boy tricking his friends into whitewashing a wall for him, *and* when crafting dark essays, such as 'To the Person Sitting in Darkness', which includes attacks on the political pieties of his day that bring to mind Yu's searing nonfiction commentaries on contemporary China. And as for that short story about the doctor with mischievous sons, well, it's easy to pretend the two youths who almost killed the surgeon were pals instead of brothers, and that their first names were Huck and Tom.

# VI

# Chicken or Beef

Growing up with no special interest in China, one of the few things I associated with the country was mix and match meal creation. On airplanes and in school cafeterias in the US, you just had 'chicken or beef' choices, but Chinese restaurants were 'one from Column A, one from Column B' combination domains. If only in recent debates on China, a similar readiness to think beyond either/or options had prevailed!

I thought of this in January 2013 when I saw a *Reuters* assessment of Xi Jinping's actions during his first few weeks of CCP leadership. The article carried this 'chicken or beef' headline: 'China's new leader: harbinger of reform or another conservative?'[25] Previous Chinese leaders had often turned out to have both reformist and conservative sides. Even Deng Xiaoping, considered the quintessential reformer due to his economic policies, held the line on political liberalisation and backed the brutal 1989 crackdown. Despite what the headline suggested, I joined with those analysts who thought it most likely that Xi, too, would end up ordering from both the reformist and conservative sides of the menu – and that is exactly what he has done.

Commentators were often falling into a similar 'chicken or beef' trap – or, rather, an 'Ai Weiwei or Zhang Yimou' one – in 2013 when dealing with creative figures. The former, who was locked into an antagonistic relationship with the government, had become the poster child for uncompromising resistance to authorities. The latter, once lauded as an edgy independent filmmaker, had taken on the role of state choreographer, overseeing the opening ceremonies of the Beijing Olympic Games and the 2009 gala commemorating the sixtieth anniversary of the founding of the PRC. Since they were two of the only internationally prominent creative Chinese figures when Mo Yan won his Nobel Prize, some commentators assumed he must either be like one or the other.

In fact, the novelist shared traits with each, but he was not all that similar to either. Like China's best-known artist, Mo had a penchant for mocking the powerful. And like the renowned filmmaker, he worked within the system. Unlike Ai Weiwei, though, Mo skewered only relatively safe targets, like the kinds of corrupt local officials that the central authorities didn't mind seeing satirised; and unlike Zhang, one of whose best films was based on the novelist's book, *Red Sorghum*, Mo had consistently produced iconoclastic works.

If Column A choices signal compliance and those from Column B indicate criticism, the artist and filmmaker were sticking to opposite sides of the menu in 2013. That said, they had not been so easy to pigeonhole at other times, for Ai Weiwei helped to design the Bird's Nest Stadium, an Olympic venue, before swerving in a radical direction just before the games opened. Zhang's early films, in contrast, sometimes ran afoul of the censors. Mo Yan, however, kept choosing from both sides of the menu. And he was not alone in doing this, for the same could have been said of other important figures, such as Jia Zhangke, the talented director who, in the early 2010s, made both envelope-pushing films that could not be shown on the mainland and a movie linked to the Shanghai Expo that was in steady rotation at the fairgrounds.

A third debate, centring on the competing predictions made by *When China Rules the World* author Martin Jacques and *The Coming Collapse of China* author Gordon G. Chang, makes me think not of combining Column A and Column B choices, but of a different feature of Chinese restaurants that I only learned about as an adult. If you don't like the options on the English language menu in some Chinatown eateries, you can ask to see a Chinese language one that lists additional dishes the proprietor doubts will interest most customers.

My problem with the Jacques vs. Chang debate is that I find neither pundit convincing. Jacques' vision of China moving smoothly toward global domination glosses over the fissures within the country's elite, as well as the many domestic challenges its government faces. Chang, on the other hand, continually underestimates the Communist Party's resiliency and adaptability. His 2001 book said it would implode by 2011. Late in 2011, he told *Foreign Policy* readers that he had miscalculated and they could 'bet on' his prophecy coming true in 2012.[26] Fast forward another half decade and we find the Party still in control – and, amazingly, Chang still being invited onto CNN to make forecasts.

When asked whether Xi Jinping is a reformer or a conservative, and whether Jia Zhangke is a collaborator or a critic, I can craft an answer that draws a bit from both Column A and Column B. Being asked whether I side with Jacques or Chang is different; I'm left feeling like a hungry vegetarian who has been given a list made up exclusively of chicken and beef dishes – and hopes desperately that there's another menu hidden in back with some acceptable choices.

# VII

# The Flat and the Bumpy

*'A spectre is haunting the world: 1914.' So writes Harold James, a professor of history [who is] certainly right that newspapers and learned journals are currently full of articles comparing international politics today with the world of 1914.*

— Gideon Rachman, 'Does the
1914 Parallel Make Sense?'
*Financial Times Blog*, 20 January, 2014[27]

*Today's China is no longer [what it was] 120 years ago.*
— Foreign Ministry Spokesperson Hua Chunying
31 December, 2013[28]

One can learn a lot about how globalisation has changed the world by considering how time was conceptualised in different places a century or so ago – for instance, at the moments flagged in these two quotes – and how it is marked now. For example, in 1900, many Chinese did not think of themselves as living on the cusp of two centuries. Neither the date '1900' nor the concept of a 'century' meant much, except to some internationally minded members of the elite, in a setting where years were described in terms of reigns and counted via references to sixty-year cycles. Now, though, in China, as in many other places, most people think of themselves as living in the middle years of the second decade of the twenty-first century.

Holidays tell a similar story, in ways that are interesting to ponder each January, as the American celebratory season ends and the biggest Chinese one is about to begin. Very few people in the China of 100 or 120 years ago thought of 25 December as a day of any special importance, nor did they associate 1 January with the start of the year. Now, however, while lunar New Year celebrations remain most important, images of Santa Claus proliferate in China's cities in late December, and Chinese friends who email me on 1 January are sure to wish me a Happy New Year. Things have reached the point where I'm sure it seemed thoroughly unremarkable when the spokeswoman for the Chinese foreign ministry ended the 31 December 2013 press briefing quoted above by wishing the journalists a 'Happy New Year' and telling them that, after a day off for the holiday, the first 2014 session would be held on 2 January.

All this would seem to fit with a way of thinking about the cultural aspects of globalisation that might be categorised as the 'Friedman Flattening' variety. This approach, which I've named in honour of New York Times columnist Thomas Friedman and his most famous book, *The World is Flat*, assumes that the dominant trend has been a smoothing out of differences. One way to symbolise this is by invoking the interchangeability of Big Macs served up wherever the golden arches soar, from Beirut to Boston, Budapest to Bangalore.

In addition, while the flattening of the world is often seen as going along with Americanisation, cultural flows from east to west can also be worked into this Friedman Flattening vision. After all, circa 1900, very few Americans (excepting those of Chinese ancestry) paid attention to the lunar New Year or the zodiacal animals associated with it. By early 2014, though, many people across the US were aware that the Year of the Horse was about to arrive. The connection between the animal and the year was even recognised by the US postal service, which issued a stamp emblazoned with a famous Chinese painting of a galloping steed.

There have always, however, been alternative views of contemporary globalisation, including one that – turning again to alliteration and to the name of a famous author – might be called 'Pico Proliferation'. This approach, named for Pico Iyer, emphasises how highly differentiated experiences remain even as fads, fashions, films, and goods move ever more rapidly around the world. To go back to McDonald's, contra the Friedman Flattening view that a Big Mac is a Big Mac is a Big Mac, a Pico Proliferating one stresses that ordering and eating this burger can mean something totally different in Tokyo as opposed to Toledo, or Managua rather than Munich.

Ever since reading *Video Night in Kathmandu – And Other Reports from the Not-So-Far East*, Iyer's seminal 1988 travelogue-cum-analysis of cultural flows in globalising times, I've known that my allegiance in this debate is firmly with Team Pico. I've periodically found ways to illustrate this in my writings, such as in a memoir-infused commentary on the strange life in global circulation of the song 'Hotel California'. This hit by The Eagles is popular in far-flung parts of the world, but often understood in distinctive ways. In both China and India, for example, it tends to be thought of as a celebratory rather than cynical take on my home state – in spite of lines likening those residing in the eponymous building to being 'prisoners' (who can 'check out any time' they like, but 'can never leave') and a menacing reference to a 'beast' being stabbed with knives.

Returning to the concept of time and holidays, the information I began with about China circa 1900 and today would ostensibly seem to fit a Friedman

Flattening vision, but on closer inspection there are Pico Proliferation dimensions aplenty. Take Santa Claus, for example: while he is now very well known in China, the jolly old elf is almost always portrayed there playing a saxophone, for unknown reasons, though his popularity rising in synch with that of the sax-playing Kenny G. could have something to do with it.

There are also differences, as well as convergences, relating to chronology. For instance, while centuries are now noted and seen as significant markers in China, this has not replaced but rather compounded the idea that sixty-year cycles are important. In 2011, the centenary of the 1911 Revolution was honoured, but two years earlier, in 2009, the sixtieth anniversary of the founding of the PRC was celebrated with the biggest National Day Parade to date. More recently still, 2013 saw events commemorating what would have been Xi Jinping's father's 100th birthday, and also lavishly marking of the passage of 120 years (a rough equivalent to a bicentennial, as it means the completion of two cycles) since Mao Zedong was born.

The continuing significance of sixty-year cycles as well as centuries in Chinese timekeeping relates to how geopolitical tensions of the present moment are being put into long-term perspective. In the United States and Europe, as noted in the first opening quote of this chapter, the final weeks of 2013 and opening weeks of

2014 saw a rash of ruminations on whether we stood at a juncture similar to that which sent us over the precipice into the horrors of World War I.

In China, though, as the second opening quote indicates, just as there are two kinds of New Year marked, there are also two kinds of 'then and now' analogies in play. Some refer to the wisdom of 1914 and 2014 parallels, while others see links and contrasts between 1894 and 2014 as more meaningful.

Just as 1914 is no ordinary year in the collective Western memory, 1894 is no ordinary year in the annals of Chinese history, as a war that began that year and ended in 1895 was the first in which Japan defeated China in a military conflict. The war in question is typically referred to in Chinese as the Jiawu War, in honour of it having taken place in a Jiawu year (the term for a Year of the Horse that matches up with the element of wood in the five elements scheme). When the official spokesperson made her comment about China now being different from 120 years ago, she did so in response to being asked to reflect on the escalating tensions between China and Japan just as an important anniversary of a major conflict between the two countries was set to arrive.

Two days later, a Beijing newspaper known for its nationalist views, the *Global Times*, elaborated on the significance of the anniversary and relevance of then-and-now analogies: 'Considering the current confrontation between both countries, Japan becomes the biggest challenge facing China. This anniversary [the 120th of the late nineteenth-century war] has already become a daunting memory in the minds of many Chinese people.'[29] It went on to stress, though, that while Japan bested China on the battlefield 120 years ago, Chinese forces went on to fight the supposedly unstoppable American army 'to a standoff' in Korea sixty years later, and the country has moved even further forward in the world since then. In 2014, more than one famous war year proved its power to haunt.

# VIII

# The People's Pope and Big Daddy Xi

In a commentary I wrote for *The Atlantic*'s website early in Xi Jinping's reign, I mused, as others had before me, on how much the Catholic Church and the CCP have in common – their obvious doctrinal differences notwithstanding. I was inspired to write the piece by a weeklong trip to Asia in March 2013, during which news broke simultaneously on opposite sides of the world of Xi's expected move from vice president to president of the PRC, and of Pope Francis's surprising selection as the new head of the Catholic Church. Two developments motivated me to revisit that theme in 2015: First, at the start of the year, the editors of the *South China Morning Post* made the curious decision to dub Xi and Francis joint winners of its inaugural 'Leader of the Year' award (they used this as an excuse to run a laudatory New Year's Day account of these two alleged proponents of bold 'reform agendas' – a move that drew praise from some readers but derision from others, with one commentator mocking the choice for being as ludicrous as the decision to give the Confucius Prize, a Chinese faux Nobel award, to Vladimir Putin in 2011). The other reason I came back to the Xi-Francis comparison was another weeklong trip abroad, this time to Rome in April 2015, which gave me a new perspective on the issue.

The thrust of my original *Atlantic* commentary was simple: when I watched news broadcasts in my Shanghai hotel room in a fuzzy, jetlagged state, I was struck by 'how hard it could be to figure out at first, when I toggled between networks or woke up from a catnap, whether a newscaster was talking about Beijing or about Rome'. There was discussion in each case of a secretive selection process being used to decide who would lead a community of roughly 1.2 billion people and head a bureaucracy with major corruption problem. There was debate over whether or not the new man would prove more of a 'reformer' than his retiring predecessor – Hu Jintao in China's case, and Pope Benedict XVI in the Vatican's – and also whether the former leader stepping aside would fade away or continue to wield influence. I concluded by noting that some of Xi's early actions as president closely paralleled those that Francis had taken as Pope. For example, both men were making gestures designed to show their commitment to simplicity and frugality. There were differences, of course, including the fact that Xi travelled with his wife, the stylish Peng Liyuan, who was acting like a typical 'First Lady', but these did not stop the parallels from clearly presenting themselves.[30]

Two years later, one thing that compelled me to revisit the comparison of the two leaders was realising, while visiting Rome, how similarly the party and the church venerate their respective leaders. Xi became general secretary of the party several months before ascending to the presidency, and then went on to accumulate many additional titles rather than just sticking to those two main posts and head of a military commission, as Hu and Jiang Zemin had done before him. This led the witty Australian sinologist Geremie Barmé to suggest a new title for him: 'Chairman of Everything'.[31] Along with more titles, Xi began to gain some of the trappings of the head of a personality cult, certainly far more than Hu and Jiang had done, and indeed even more than Deng Xiaoping, the strongest and most revered leader since Mao. By spring 2015, one of Xi's catchphrases, 'The Chinese Dream', was being featured on countless street posters, and his face was showing up in many places, including bookstores, where it was common to see stacks of tomes by and about him.

When I arrived in Rome early in April 2015, since I had just been in Shanghai three months before, the signs of rising Xi-mania were fresh in my mind. In China, the reminders and images of the Chairman of Everything were everywhere. In Rome, the likenesses of the current Pope were just as ubiquitous – and not just when I visited Vatican City late in the week. At souvenir carts and in shop windows near tourist areas, Francis's face appeared on refrigerator magnets, calendar covers, and even on bobble head dolls. In photographs, he is shown giving a thumbs-up sign to the viewer, reinforcing the notion that 'Papa Francesco' is an informal man of the people. This imagery of a religious leader sometimes called 'The People's Pope' matches some of the portrayals of his Chinese counterpart, a man often referred to now as 'Xi Dada' (Big Papa Xi).

A close look at displays of papal-themed mementos brought to light a shared trait of the two organisations that I hadn't considered before: former heads of each are not venerated equally. Every Pope may be honoured in his day, but just as you see more images of Mao and Deng than of Hu and Jiang in Xi's China, you see many more trinkets emblazoned with the faces of some of Francis's precursors than you do of Benedict XVI. This fits with the fact that only some former Popes are made saints, and two of Francis's predecessors, John Paul II and John XXIII, made the grade. There is also, as I learned while touring Vatican City, a spillover to this difference with regards to burial. While the standard practice is to bury Popes *beneath* St. Peter's Basilica, there is a second burial, linked to beatification, in which the bodies of especially sacred Popes are interred *above ground* in a special section of that massive church.

The CCP, being an atheist organisation, doesn't have official 'saints', but it does have counterparts to beatification. There are famous 'revolutionary martyrs', for example, who inspire hagiographic treatments in print and other media, and, like saints, have statues and monuments made in their honour. There are also some past Chinese leaders who get elevated in ways that bring to mind Popes who become 'saints' or, in very rare cases, rise even higher posthumously and have the honorific 'great' added to their names. Deng, despite some misguided actions, has been celebrated posthumously in ways that bring to mind a Pope who became a saint; his celebrated role in laying the groundwork for China's economic boom is, in this comparison, equivalent to the 'miracle' needed for beatification. Mao, despite the horrific results of some of his policies, would be the obvious candidate for the party's equivalent to a 'great' saint. This is due to the role that the chairman, also known as 'The Great Helmsman', played in the miraculous Long March and the founding of the PRC.

It is worth noting that only Mao's body, not Deng's, lies in a mausoleum that serves as a pilgrimage site in the heart of Tiananmen Square, not far from the

Monument to the People's Heroes – an obelisk surrounded by marble friezes that pays homage to the revolutionary martyrs who helped Mao accomplish his miracles. Criticism of Deng is often kept in check; one reason for the taboo on publicly discussing 1989's June Fourth massacre is that doing so reflects badly on him. Still, this is nothing compared to the way that, at various times, speaking or writing about Mao in certain ways is deemed blasphemous, and some news broke while I was in Rome that offered fresh evidence of that fact. The story was: a television host was censured for dissing the Great Helmsman at a banquet. While, as a *New York Times* reporter noted, the diss itself may be common enough in private, it is verboten in any public setting.[32]

Touring Vatican City, I saw many specific things that brought to mind parallels of the allegedly secular but actually sacred sites of central Beijing. For example, St Peter's Square and Tiananmen Square are both near museums. Both are vast plazas where crowds sometimes gather at ritually important moments – Easter, for example, in the former case, and National Day in the latter. More specifically, the combination of statues of saints arrayed above St. Peter's Square and the obelisk at which they seem to be gazing seems in some ways a deconstructed counterpart to Tiananmen's Monument to the People's Heroes. The main difference is that, in the case of the Beijing monolith, the images of the 'saints' are etched in marble on its side rather than physically separated from it.

Perhaps the single object that made the deepest impression on me, though, was *The School of Athens*, a famous work by Raphael that is among the Vatican Museum's great treasures. In this painting, which visitors see just before entering the Sistine Chapel, Raphael celebrates the accomplishments of great thinkers from the past, including the philosophers Socrates, Plato, and Aristotle, all of whom lived centuries before the birth of Christ.

To explain why this painting made such an impression, I need to note that two days before seeing it, I had been thinking about the relationship between China's Communist Party and Confucius, who lived about a century before Socrates. The Chinese sage had been on my mind because of a presentation I had given on Hong Kong's Umbrella Movement at Rome's La Sapienza University, hosted by the school's Oriental Studies department. La Sapienza happens to be home to what is now the longest established Confucius Institute in Europe – a title it claimed after the closing of the very first continental Confucius Institute in Stockholm, Sweden. Arriving early for my talk, I strolled around the Oriental Studies Institute's courtyard and saw a large statue of Confucius – the sort you often come across in foreign locales where there are Confucius Institutes, and also sometimes find now in China in various places, including on campuses, near public libraries, and, though it only stood there for a short period, in Tiananmen Square itself. Seeing that statue, I decided to open my talk with a digression. I noted that I begin *China in the 21st Century: What Everyone Needs to Know*, which is in question and answer format, with an examination of Confucius's beliefs. I move on to ask whether Confucius has always been revered in China, and answer that he hasn't. I stress that Mao – the most famous and infamous leader of the same Communist Party that now proudly funds Confucius Institutes around the world – was a harsh critic of the sage; once in power, he even launched campaigns aimed at ridding the country of all lingering vestiges of Confucianism.

*The School of Athens* has altered my perspective on the Communist Party's relationship to Confucius. There is no anti-Aristotle campaign in the Church's history similar to the one Mao waged against Confucius, but there were points when the early Church banned some of his writings. Raphael's painting reminds us, however, that by the Renaissance, things like this could be overlooked – much as Mao's criticisms of Confucius are in China today. My tour through the Vatican made me realise that Xi's lionising of Mao in one breath and then quoting Confucius in the next may not be quite as strange as I once considered it to be.

The months following my trip to Rome offered many reminders of the need to keep from overextending the parallels between Xi and Pope Francis. For example, Xi made headlines in September 2015 by presiding over a nationalistic military parade, while, during the period leading up to and immediately following that jingoistic martial spectacle, the People's Pope made pronouncements on climate change and the need for compassion toward refugees – declarations that were globally minded and the opposite of militaristic.

Still, even if the future offers more examples of the two men's divergent paths, I expect to occasionally come across articles about the People's Pope that, with just a bit of alteration, could have been describing the Chairman of Everything – or vice versa. Like, for instance, a *National Catholic Reporter* editorial that was published on 23 March 2015, but which I did not come across until after returning from Rome. Though it focused on the Pope, the article's title could have easily served as the heading for a piece on Xi, if just the last word had been altered: 'What Kind of Reformer is Francis?' The opening line, too, would have worked well in an essay on China with only minor word changes: 'Any assessment of Pope Francis at the two-year mark of his papacy would do best to first deal with the unrealistic expectations and the disappointments that often drive the discussion over whether he is a true reformer.'[33] It is then explained that, while Francis had made dramatic moves to rein in bureaucratic abuses, his policies were completely in line with his predecessors' when it came to the status of women in the church hierarchy as well as some other issues. All of which goes to show that it is not only in China that we find leaders dubbed 'reformers' ordering from both the reformist and traditionalist sides of the menu.

Here I must stress that it is too soon to answer some questions about the limits and value of Xi-Francis comparisons. For example, we will not know until well after Francis dies – as the Western saying goes, has gone to 'meet his maker' – whether he will be posthumously treated as an ordinary former Pope or be sanctified. We will get clues about Xi's ultimate symbolic status in China's leadership lineage by noting how his slogans, books and memorabilia fare after he is no longer the Chairman of Everything. But we won't be certain of that status until Xi has not just retired but passed on – or, in the Chinese Communist parlance, gone to 'meet Marx'. Then again, perhaps in his case we should say gone to 'meet Marx and Confucius', as he would surely not consider his death complete if he was greeted only by the German philosopher and not also by the Chinese sage.

# NOTES

1. Howard W. French, 'Beijing's claims of an unwavering stand in Tibet are groundless', *International Herald Tribune*, 20 March, 2008; and Pankaj Mishra, 'At war with the utopia of modernity', *Guardian*, 22 March, 2008.
2. 'China Garners Broad International Support Over Tibet Riots', *Xinhua News Agency*, 22 March, 2008.
3. 'Bush offers Hu condolences, US unveils quake aid', *Agence France-Presse* (AFP), 15 May, 2008.
4. John W. Dower, 'A warning from history: Don't expect democracy in Iraq', *Boston Review*, February/March 2003; see also idem, 'Why Iraq is not Japan . . .' *TomDispatch.com*, 29 April, 2003, and 'The other Japanese occupation', *TomDispatch.com*, 20 June, 2003.
5. Dower, 'The other Japanese occupation'.
6. William Davies, 'Is it Aldous Huxley or George Orwell?' *New Statesman*, 1 August, 2005.
7. Stuart McMillen, 'Amusing ourselves to death', Recombinant Records: Cartoons by Stuart McMillen, 24 May, 2009, online at http://www.recombinantrecords.net/2009/05/24/amusing-our-selves-to-death/ (accessed 23 October, 2015).
8. George Orwell, 'To S. Moos', 16 November, 1943, in *George Orwell: A Life in Letters* (New York: Norton, 2013), p. 217.
9. This letter is quoted at length in Jeffrey Meyers, *Orwell: Wintry Conscience of a Generation* (New York: Norton, 2001), pp. 288–289, one of many works that refers to Huxley having taught Orwell at Eton.
10. William Gibson, 'Disneyland with the death penalty', *Wired*, 1 April, 1993.
11. Charles Horner, *Rising China and Its Postmodern Fate* (Athens, GA: University of Georgia Press, 2009), p. 4.
12. Jonathan Jones, 'Ai Weiwei isn't on trial: China is', *Guardian*, 14 April, 2011.

13   Michael Wines, 'In restive Chinese area, cameras keep watch', *New York Times*, 2 August, 2010.
14   Barbara Demick, *Nothing to Envy: Ordinary Lives in North Korea*. (New York: Spiegel and Grau, 2009), p. 281.
15   David Remnick, 'The civil archipelago', *New Yorker*, 19 December, 2011.
16   Evan Osnos, *Age of Ambition: Chasing Fortune, Truth, and Faith in the New China*, (New York: FSG, 2014).
17   Evan Osnos, 'The age of complacency?' *New Yorker*, 27 July, 2010.
18   Evan Osnos, 'Looking beyond ethnicity', *New Yorker*, 8 July, 2009; and 'Xinjiang: the reckoning begins', *New Yorker*, 9 July, 2009.
19   Alison Flood, 'Salman Rushdie defends his right to call Mo Yan a "patsy"', *Guardian*, 17 December, 2012.
20   Sabina Knight, 'Mo Yan's delicate balancing act', *National Interest*, no. 124, March-April 2013, pp. 69–80.
21   See Pankaj Mishra, 'Why Salman Rushdie should stick to holding Obama to account', *Guardian*, 4 January 2013; see also the comments by Mishra and several others on the Mo Yan Nobel Prize win in the February 2014 issue of *Guernica*.
22   Selina Lai-Henderson, *Mark Twain in China* (Stanford: Stanford University Press, 2015), p. 60.
23   Amy Qin, 'The curious, and continuing, appeal of Mark Twain in China', *New York Times*, 6 January, 2014.
24   Yu Hua, *Boy in the Twilight*, trans. Allan H. Barr (New York: Pantheon Books, 2014), p. 68.
25   Terrill Yue Jones and Benjamin Kang Lim, 'China's new leader: harbinger of reform or another conservative?' *Reuters*, 10 January, 2013.
26   Gordon G. Chang, 'The coming collapse of China: 2012 edition', *Foreign Policy*, 29 December, 2011.
27   Gideon Rachman, 'Does the 1914 parallel make sense?' *Financial Times Blog*, 20 January, 2014.
28   'Foreign ministry spokesperson Hua Chunying's regular press conference on December 31, 2013', Consulate General of the People's Republic of China in CEBU, 31 December, 2013, http://cebu.china-consulate.org/eng/fyrth/t1113606.htm (last accessed 23 October, 2015).
29   'War of 120 years ago offer lessons for today', *Global Times*, 2 January, 2014.
30   Jeffrey Wasserstrom, 'The Vatican and the Chinese Communist Party: more similar than you think', *Atlantic* website, 3 April 2013, http://www.theatlantic.com/china/archive/2013/04/the-

vatican-and-the-chinese-communist-party-more-similar-than-you-think/274596/ (last accessed October 23, 2015).
31  One of many works to credit Barmé with the nickname is Andrew Browne, 'The whiplash of Xi Jinping's top-down style', *Wall Street Journal*, 23 June, 2015.
32  Chris Buckley, 'Joking about Mao lands Chinese TV host in hot water', *New York Times*, 10 April 2015.
33  NCR Editorial staff, 'Editorial: What kind of reformer is Francis?' *National Catholic Reporter*, 23 March, 2015.

# ACKNOWLEDGEMENTS

This may be a slender volume, but writing the preceding pages has led me to accumulate many debts. I want to thank, first of all, two people at Penguin China. One is Chen Mengfei, who first suggested to a former professor turned friend that he consider reworking some of his essays into a volume that could be published as a 'special' by her employers. The other is Imogen Liu, who provided invaluable guidance at each stage, which led to an imagined book becoming an actual one. I also need to acknowledge a debt to the many talented and patient editors who worked with me to shape eight short commentaries published between 2008 and 2015; those commentaries, in adapted and expanded form, became the main chapters of this volume. For help with Chapter 1, which is based on a piece that appeared in *openDemocracy* in 2008, I am grateful to David Hayes; for Chapter 2, which expands on themes explored in an essay written for *Foreign Policy*, I am grateful to Christina Larson; and for Chapter 6, which is derived from a contribution to the Oxford University Press blog,

I am grateful to Christian Purdy. Chapters 3, 4, 5, 7, and 8 all evolved out of contributions to the *Los Angeles Review of Books*; they benefited from the editorial work of the following people: Jonathan Hahn (whose input on the essay dealing with Xi Jinping and Pope Francis was particularly valuable), Chris Heiser, Evan Kindley, Tom Lutz (the publication's visionary founder), Megan Shank, and Laurie Winer (who did so much to help sharpen my thinking about Yu Hua and Mark Twain). I also want to thank the editors at *cinaforum*, who published an Italian version of Chapter 8 at the same time that the English language one ran in the *LARB*.

I want to express my gratitude as well to the following friends and colleagues who read and commented on one or more chapters early in their creation: Perry Anderson, Alec Ash, Allan Barr, Jay Carter, Alexis Dudden, Harriet Evans, Howard French, Sabina Knight, Lee Haiyan, Pankaj Mishra, Benjamin Nathans, Emily Rosenberg, Angilee Shah, Brooke Thomas, Jeff Veidlinger, Wang Chaohua, and Tim Weston. Maria Bucur, Stephen Platt and Anjali Vaidya were good enough to look at and make suggestions about the whole manuscript when I wanted it assessed by fresh eyes. I owe a lot to four people who have continually made time in recent years to read even very rough drafts of essays and give me frank reactions to them as well as valuable suggestions for improvement: Maura Cunningham, Ian Johnson, Julia Lovell, and

Kate Merkel-Hess. In addition, the first places that I try out analogies are in classrooms, at public talks, and in conversations in Irvine, either on the campus or at home. The reactions I get in these different settings tell me which juxtapositions are worth running with and which are not. For responses to ideas I floated on campus, I am grateful to the graduate and undergraduate students I have taught in recent years, and to Jennifer Munger, Kavita Philip, Ken Pomeranz, Jon Wiener, Amy Wilentz, and Laura Mitchell; for responses at home, heartfelt thanks, as in all my previous books, to Anne Bock.

**PENGUIN SPECIALS**

# Cathay: Ezra Pound's Orient

IRA NADEL

'Pound is the inventor of Chinese poetry for our time.' – T.S. Eliot

---

At the turn of the twentieth century, London was a breeding ground for the avant-garde. Modernist writers like T.S. Eliot, W.B. Yeats and Ezra Pound became infatuated with the Orient. Pound in particular was inspired by the clarity and precision of Eastern poetry to rethink the nature of an English poem. Published in 1915, Cathay, Pound's collection of fourteen experimental translations of classic Chinese poems, was a groundbreaking work that set the stage for a new-found East in the West.

Ira Nadel is a biographer and literary critic, and currently serves as Distinguished University Professor in the Department of English, University of British Columbia. He is a Fellow of the Royal Society of Canada and was awarded the 1996 Medal for Canadian Biography. He has written biographies of Leonard Cohen, Tom Stoppard and Ezra Pound and published extensively on Joyce and the subject of biography.

---

www.penguin.com.cn

> PENGUIN
> SPECIALS

# What's Wrong with Diplomacy?

## KERRY BROWN

**The Future of Diplomacy and the Case of China and the UK**

Traditional methods of diplomacy are fast becoming antiquated. Secrecy, pomp and elitism may have dictated diplomatic strategy of the Cold War era, but in a digitised twenty-first century, inclusivity and transparency are values of increasing importance. Access to information is being democratised for a global citizenry, and nowadays everyone is a potential diplomat. From the handover of Hong Kong to recent high-profile political scandal, former diplomat Kerry Brown explores the chequered relationship between the UK and China, offering fresh insights into the fraught and ever-changing dynamic between these two countries. What's Wrong with Diplomacy? is a call to arms and a probing indictment of diplomacy's failure to adapt to a changing world

---

Kerry Brown is Professor of Chinese Studies and Director of the Lau China Institute at King's College, London. He is an Associate Fellow on the Asia Programme at Chatham House, London, and served in the British Foreign and Commonwealth Office from 1998 to 2005. Brown is the author of over ten books, the most recent being *The New Emperors: Power* and the *Princelings in China*.

'Part memoir, part advocacy, Kerry Brown's compelling and provocative essay is a clarion call for a change in the UK's diplomatic practices.' - *Professor Rosemary Foot, PhD, FBA, Department of Politics and International Relations, St Antony's College, University of Oxford*

'Brown's call for a more modern, diverse and transparent approach to diplomatic engagement in the information age is worthwhile reading for anyone interested in Britain's relations with China.' - *Duncan Hewitt, Adjunct Professor, New York University, Shanghai, and author of Getting Rich First: Life in a Changing China*